Very Silly Country

Steve Barlow and Steve Skidmore

Illustrated by
Andy Hammond

OXFORD
UNIVERSITY PRESS

"I hate cross-country running," said Tim.

"So do I," said Ben.

"It's not fair," said Tim. "It's too wet to go for a run."

Tim and Ben got very wet and very cross. They were not good at running. That is why they didn't like cross-country running.

"Can you see the rest of the class?" asked Ben.

"They are way ahead," said Tim.

"I have to stop," said Ben. "I feel sick."
He was.

"It's not fair! I'm always last," said Ben. "I want to be first!"

"I have a plan," said Tim. "I think we can get back first."
"How?" asked Ben.

"If we go across that field," said Tim. "We'll be back first! No one will find out."

The field was very muddy and full of cow pats.

"These cow pats smell," said Ben.

"Just don't step in them!" said Tim.

"Look!" said Ben. "It's a cow."
Tim looked. "That's not a cow," he said. "That's a bull! And he's coming for us!"

RUN!!!

Tim and Ben ran for their lives!
Now they were good at running!
"Which way?" yelled Ben.
"Go for the gate," said Tim.

The bull was very near. The bull ran fast. Tim and Ben ran very fast. They got to the gate first. They jumped onto it.

But the bull didn't stop. It hit the gate.

Tim and Ben fell into a cow pat.
They got very wet and very smelly!

The rest of the class ran past.
Tim and Ben were not going to be first. They were going to be last.